MAKE THIS!

FANTASIA

UNDER THE SEA

With SCRATCH-OFF PAGES to create COLOURFUL MERMAID ART

ABOUT THIS BOOK

Fantastical fun!

This activity book is full of things to do! There are pages to colour in and lots of fun activities for you to complete.

Then, when you've finished all of that, there are four pages of gorgeous scratch art for you to create!

HOW TO CREATE YOUR SCRATCH ART

Put your scratch art page on a flat surface, to make scratching easier. Use your scratch art tool to trace around the outlines of the picture. The colours underneath will show through wherever you scratch. Press down firmly as you scratch so as much colour as possible is revealed. Then, keep scratching to create lots of different patterns inside the outlines – try crosshatches, stripes, zigzags, or even spots or stars!

SPOT THE DIFFERENCE

Sea life!

Can you spot the difference in each pair? Check your answers at the back of this book.

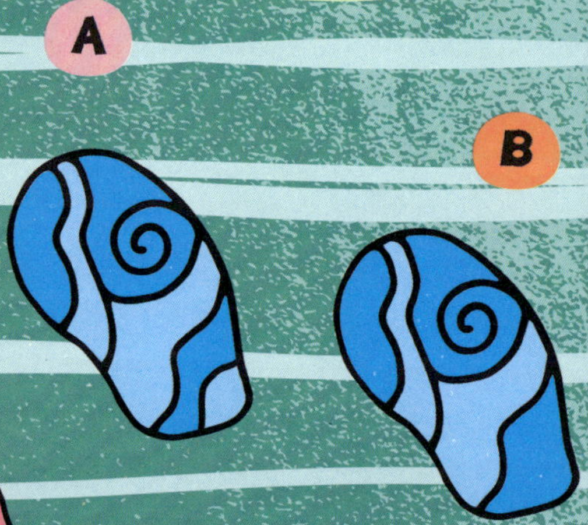

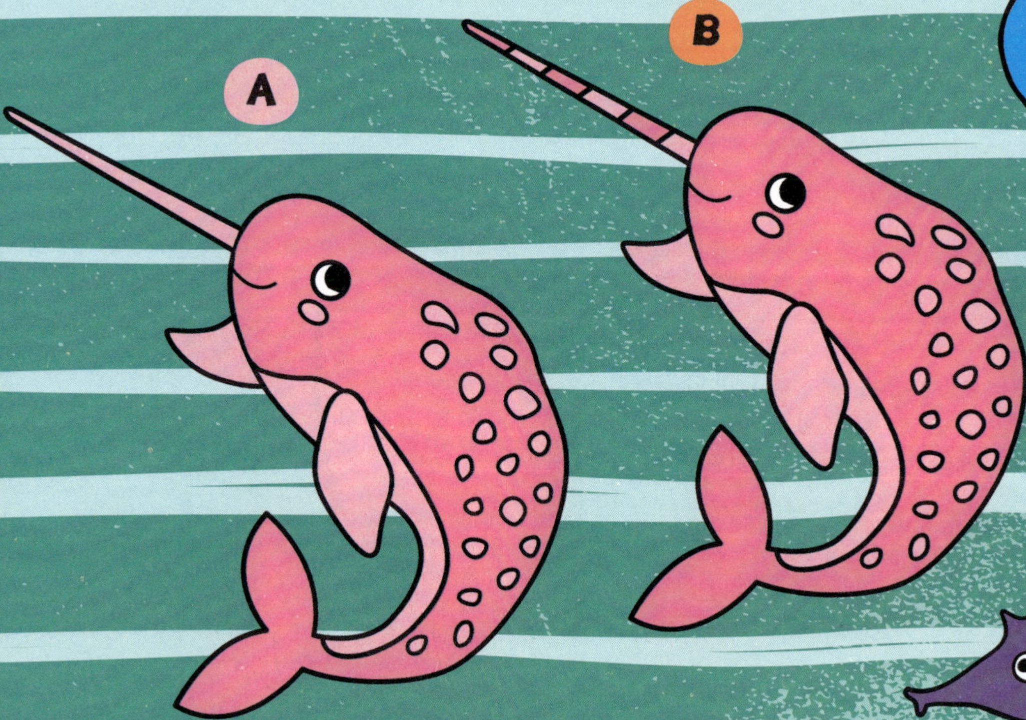

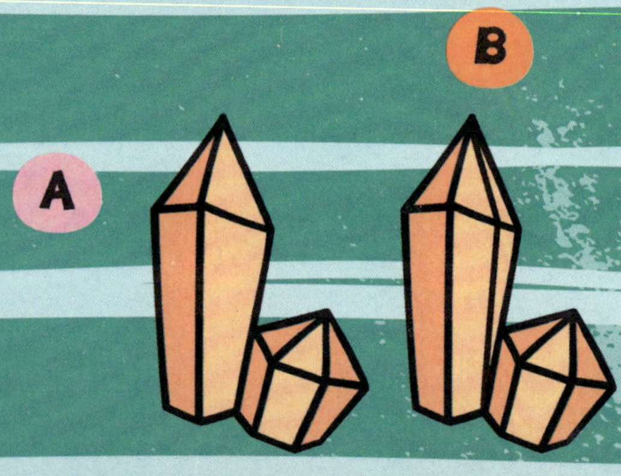

STARFISH MAZE

It's starfish time!
Find your way through the starfish maze.

CORAL CROSSWORD

Under the sea!

Read the clues to complete the crossword.

		1. M						
2. C		R						
				3. S				
	4. F	I		H				
	5. W			L				

ACROSS

2. Colourful and grows on the seabed.
3. Has sharp teeth and a fin that sticks out of the water.
4. Swims in the sea.
5. The largest mammal in the sea.

DOWN

1. Part-fish, part-woman.
3. Little creatures live in them and you can find them on the sand.

ODD ONE OUT

Pretty shells!

Circle the odd one out in each row and then check your answers at the back of this book.

A

B

C

D

FISH SUDOKU

Cute fish!

Use the pictures below to fill in the blank squares and complete the sudoku puzzle. Only one of each picture can be used in each row and column. Check your answers at the back of the book.

CRACK THE CODE

Mermaid madness!

Each letter of the alphabet is matched to a picture. Look at the pictures and crack the code to find a message!

COLOURING FUN

OCEAN WORD SEARCH

Play in the sea!
See if you can find these words in the word search.

O	C	E	A	N	A	T	R	O
N	S	T	R	I	L	R	S	M
C	E	N	U	N	I	E	T	E
H	A	C	R	A	B	A	A	R
J	H	P	M	Q	B	S	R	M
K	O	V	O	E	A	U	F	A
W	R	X	E	I	U	R	I	I
S	S	A	N	D	A	E	S	D
A	E	T	S	P	H	G	H	D

MERMAID
OCEAN
SEAHORSE
SAND
TREASURE
CRAB
STARFISH

A-MAZE-ING WHALE

Whale watching!

Which path will lead the boat to the whale?

PATTERN PUFFERFISH

Pufferfish is crazy for patterns!
Help Pufferfish figure out which object comes next in each row to complete the pattern.

SEALIFE SEARCH

Which is which?

Draw a line from each sea creature to its matching shadow.

TRICKY PUZZLE

Jigsaw fun!

Circle the jigsaw piece that belongs in the blank space.

WAVY WORD SEARCH

Fishy fun!

See if you can find these words in the word search.

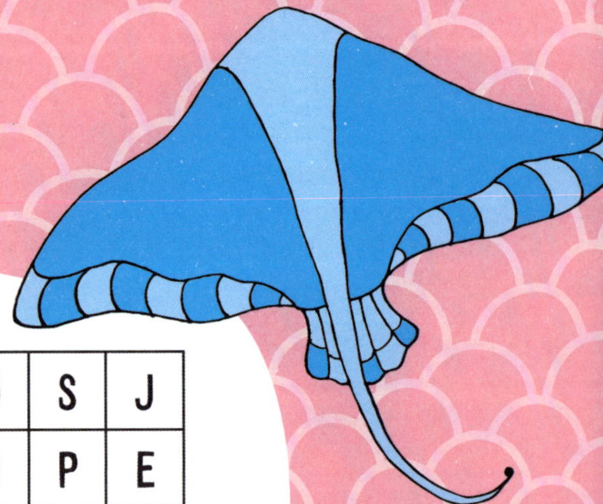

B	O	C	T	O	P	U	S	J
A	S	N	T	E	R	D	P	E
E	H	T	F	H	N	O	A	L
U	A	B	U	B	B	L	E	L
W	R	I	P	C	S	P	E	Y
B	K	T	Y	D	K	H	N	F
T	U	R	T	L	E	I	M	I
Y	V	J	L	U	A	N	O	S
S	T	I	N	G	R	A	Y	H

DOLPHIN
TURTLE
OCTOPUS
BUBBLE
JELLYFISH
SHARK
STINGRAY

SANDY SUDOKU

Shelly creatures!

Use the pictures below to fill in the blank squares and complete the sudoku puzzle. Only one of each picture can be used in each row and column. Check your answers at the back of the book.

COLOUR ME IN!

BOAT DOUBLES

Double trouble!

Which two boats are identical?

CUTE SEA FRIENDS

Let's meet!

The cute little crab wants to visit her friends. Which path should she take?

CRACK THE CODE

Pirate treasure

Each letter of the alphabet is matched to a picture. Look at the pictures and crack the code to find a secret message!

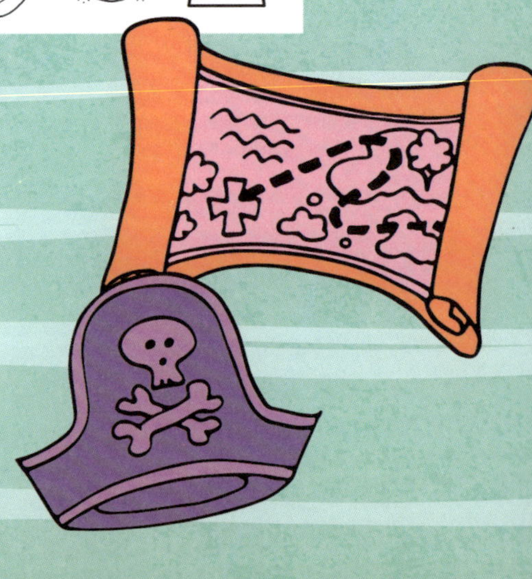

SHELL PATTERNS

Which shells?

Look at the patterns on the right. Then, choose the correct box of shells on the left to fill the blank space.

A

B

C

MERMAID MATHS MAZE

Pretty mermaid!

Follow the numbers to help the mermaid find the starfish.

		32	2	2	28	27	26	25	10	
FINISH		←	31	30	29	23	9	24	29	
16	18	16	10	8	17	24	6	23	10	
17	21	19	14	11	19	20	21	22	11	
13	14	15	16	17	18	19	7	12	10	
12	9	13	12	18	10	9	8			
11	10	9	8	11	12	5	6			
16	19	15	7	9	10	7	4			
14	13	10	6	13	2	1	←	START		
12	11	8	5	4	3	6	10			

DOLPHIN FUN

Cute as pie!

Use the grid to copy this dolphin!

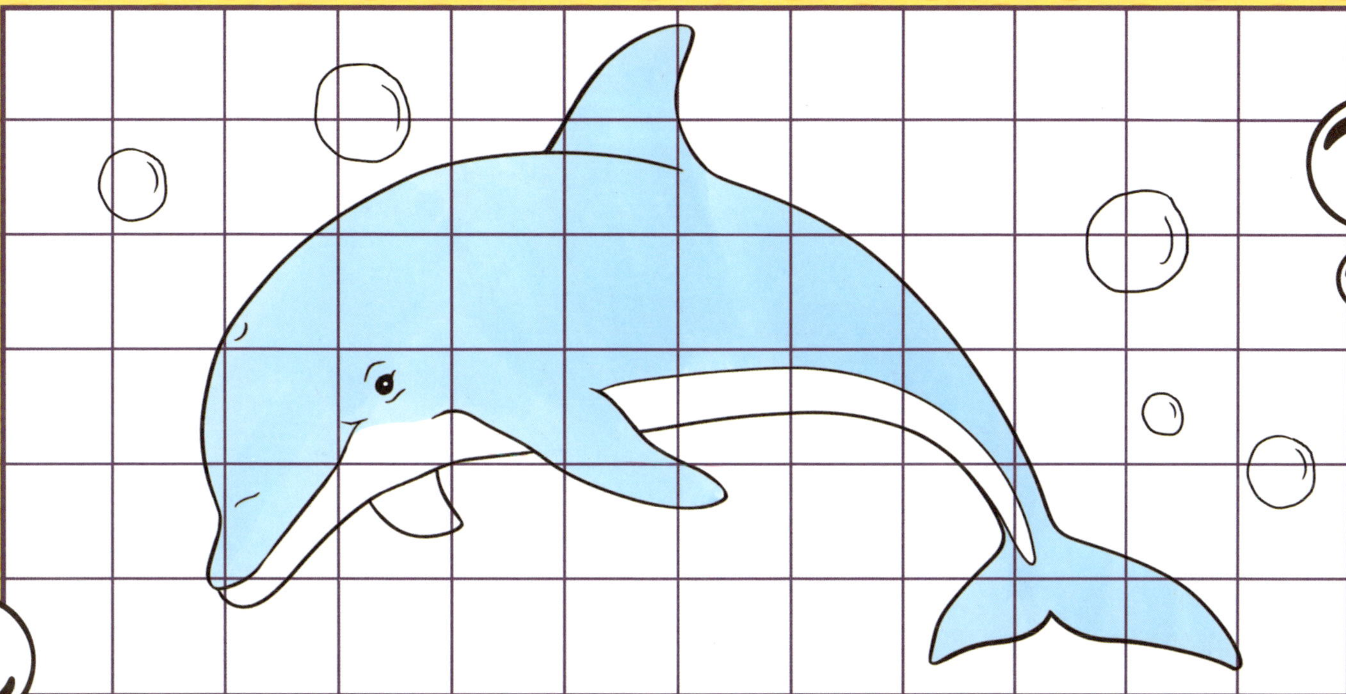

COLOURING FUN

SANDY CROSSWORD

Hidden treasure!
Read the clues to complete the crossword.

ACROSS

2. You sit on it at the beach.
4. A horse that lives in the sea.
5. A fish made of jelly that you can't eat!
6. It has a hard shell.

DOWN

1. You can surf on it.
3. You might find jewels in it.

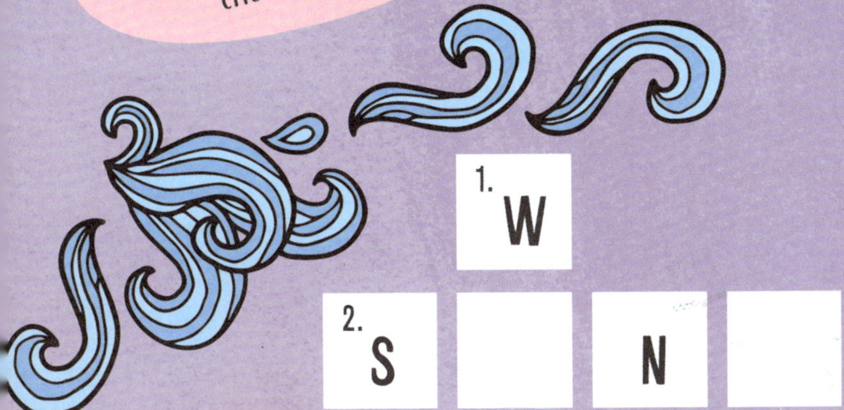

ANSWERS

PAGE 4

PAGE 5

PAGE 6

PAGE 7

PAGE 8

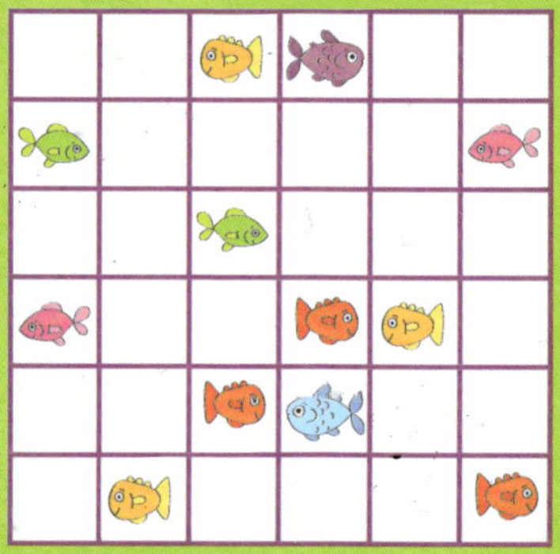

PAGE 9

MERMAIDS SING SWEET SONGS!

PAGE 11

O	C	E	A	N	A	T	R	O
N	S	T	R	I	L	R	S	M
C	E	N	U	N	I	E	T	E
H	A	C	R	A	B	A	A	R
J	H	P	M	Q	B	S	R	M
K	O	V	O	E	A	U	F	A
W	R	X	E	I	U	R	I	I
S	S	A	N	D	A	E	S	D
A	E	T	S	P	H	G	H	D

PAGE 12

C

PAGE 13

PAGE 14

PAGE 15

PAGE 16

B	O	C	T	O	P	U	S	J
A	S	N	T	E	R	D	P	E
E	H	T	F	H	N	O	A	L
U	A	B	U	B	B	L	E	L
W	R	I	P	C	S	P	E	Y
B	K	T	Y	D	K	H	N	F
T	U	R	T	L	E	I	M	I
Y	V	J	L	U	A	N	O	S
S	T	I	N	G	R	A	Y	H

PAGE 17

PAGE 20

A + G

PAGE 21

B

PAGE 22

I FOUND THE TREASURE!

PAGE 23

B

PAGE 27

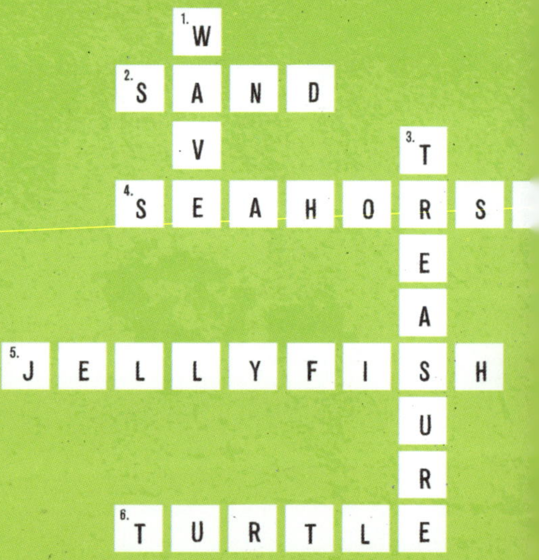